MORTGAGE PEACE

A Proven Formula for a Smooth On-Time Closing

Stephanie A. Weeks

Mortgage Peace

A Proven Formula for a Smooth On-Time Closing

Copyright © 2016 Stephanie A. Weeks

All rights reserved.

CONTENTS

Introduction 5

Chapter 1: Understanding 9

Chapter 2: Protect Yourselves 13

Chapter 3: Peace Of Mind 29

Chapter 4: The Ultimate Understanding Of The Underwriting Process, With The End Goal In Mind: A Smooth And Peaceful Transaction 31

Chapter 5: Different Types Of Income: You Need What Document From Me? 39

Chapter 6: A Winning Team 47

Chapter 7: Closing—The Moving Truck 61

Chapter 8: In Conclusion 65

INTRODUCTION

My name is Stephanie Weeks, and I've been a mortgage lender for more than 13 years. I've been extremely successful and happy with all the customers who I've been able to help, but I felt a calling to make more of an impact.

Lending is constantly changing, and the information is overwhelming and unclear. However, the biggest challenge is that consumers *don't know what they don't know.*

After a futile search for books to help my clients understand the lending process, I continually came up empty-handed. Then I realized it was my duty to write a book. You see, my mission is to change the world, one loan at a time.

I've written this book to transform the mortgage industry and help every potential homebuyer, seller, investor, and/or person refinancing.

This book is to help you learn what you don't know and better understand the process so you can protect yourself as a consumer.

The vast majority of consumers financing homes have a negative experience rather than a positive one. With this book, I intend to change that.

In the United States, there are millions of mortgage transactions every year. Unfortunately, 70 percent of mortgage loans do not close on time or are denied at the last moment, leaving a trail of devastation.

A study by the Federal National Mortgage Association (commonly known as Fannie Mae) showed that the majority of all mortgage loans close late. What if that could be changed? It's not impossible. An on-time closing can be achieved in three simple steps:

- Educate the consumers.
- Clarify the process.
- Implement systems.

This book will give you the knowledge and power to secure the best deal and achieve your goal of a smooth, on-time closing.

I can't tell you how many times I've heard people complaining about how clueless they felt regarding their mortgage process. Most borrowers simply don't know what's happening, or what should be happening.

This book will answer your questions and teach you what you should know. I want to save people the heartache and wasted energy that comes from trying to operate within this system without being informed.

I want everyone to remember that each loan represents an individual or individuals or a family. It is not just a "loan." It's a life or lives.

For example, imagine being several months pregnant, sitting in a moving truck, headed to your closing. You have already sold your previous house and you were told that you didn't need any more cash to close; aside from the deposit you've already given.

You are literally en route to the closing when you get a call and somebody says, "Hi! You need another $7,000 to close."

What do you do in that moment? Everything you own is on that truck and you don't have another $7,000. Panic sets in as you worry if you're about to become homeless. Unfortunately, these calls are not uncommon. This happened to me before I became a lender. It was quite traumatic.

My personal lending "horror" stories prior to being a lender are partial inspiration for writing this book. I want to protect consumers from what has happened to me and what I have seen happen with other lenders.

If you read this book and follow my system for reaching a stress-free closing, you can avoid having your whole life on a truck with nowhere to unload it.

Let me ask you a few simple questions. Do you want to:

- Close on time?
- Guarantee that you get the best loan officer available?
- Pay only the costs you MUST to borrow the money and avoid paying any extras?
- Eliminate surprises along the way?
- Be confident and worry-free during the application process and closing?
- Go to the closing day with total confidence that it will be a smooth process and you will understand what you're signing?

If you said yes to these questions, then you are in the right place! I am excited that you have chosen me to be your guide on this journey toward the largest investment you might make in your lifetime. Let's get started!

CHAPTER 1

UNDERSTANDING

Successful Lending Requires Teamwork

The primary point to remember regarding your loan is that teamwork makes the dream work!

When you're thinking about a loan, imagine that I, as a loan officer, have to put together a 1,000-piece puzzle. Keep in mind, I do not know what the final picture even looks like. I just have to make the pieces fit perfectly and create the picture.

However, in order for me to put it together, I also have to participate in a scavenger hunt to find all the pieces! That's essentially what lenders and loan officers have to do. And if any piece of the puzzle is missing, or even late, then you will not get the loan.

If I say to a consumer, "I need your tax returns. I need every page and every schedule," the client might only send in the first page of the tax return, saying, "This shows you all the totals that you need. Why do you need more? That should work."

However, lenders do not work from totals. We need to analyze all the numbers—all the lines, all the details. Also, yes, that first page does show the total for W-2 income, but it doesn't explain if it was from one job or five jobs or if it was from one person on the return or both—just as an example.

We need every page, every Form W-2 (Wage and Tax Statement), Form 1099 (Miscellaneous Income), Schedule K-1 for business income (if applicable), and every Internal Revenue Service (IRS) form and schedule to put all the pieces of the puzzle together.

Often lenders will get pushback from borrowers who own various businesses or have spouses operating side businesses at a loss that they forget to mention. Or they might resist submitting their K-1 or 1099 if they don't feel it's relevant.

By all means, ask questions. I want you to understand every part of the process, but please know that until we have every single document we've requested, it's as if we have no documents.

I'm responsible for putting the puzzle together, but you actually have all the pieces, so we have to work together as a team.

A loan closing smoothly comes down to teamwork between the borrower and the loan officer. It never fails; the quickest closings are the result of the most compliant customers.

Teamwork Requires Flexibility

I remember when I was buying my first house. My husband and I were on one side of the desk, the builder was on the other, and I said, "We need the payment to be $500 a month because we're paying $400 now and I know we can afford $500. I don't mean $520 or $550. I need it to be $500."

The builder leaned back in his chair and he said, "Darling, your payment is going to be $530, and if you're worried about 30 bucks, you ain't ready to buy a house." It's difficult to settle on a precise amount in the beginning, because you might not know all the variables. Lesson: As a borrower, remember to be a little flexible.

Being flexible regarding the proposed payment is important. For example, do you need flood insurance? How much is the policy? Having home insurance is a given, but the type and cost of the policy will vary depending on the age, size, and style of the house. The list of variables is detailed. Your job is to be educated.

It's not uncommon for lenders to only give clients the principal and interest amount, never mentioning the various taxes and insurances costs—online calculations are notorious for this. As an informed consumer, you'll make sure that your total includes the principal, interest, and property tax, plus all required home and mortgage insurance estimates. Don't forget homeowner association (HOA) dues, if applicable.

At the same time, do allow for a slight margin of error. The loan officer is predicting all the variables—the location of your home, the exact cost, and so on. Remaining flexible, checking for missing items, and asking questions are key ingredients of good teamwork.

The Five Mistakes that Most Borrowers Make and How to Avoid Them

1. Remember that it is in the "interest" of the lender to secure a loan for you. The lenders don't make money unless they give you a loan.

2. Don't assume that all lenders know what will be a good fit for you. Some are inexperienced, while others are merely good salespeople, only competent in getting your business. They might not be good at securing the best loan for you or providing the best service or most accurate details.

3. Don't let the loan officer interview you; understand that you are there to interview him or her. Would you hire a financial advisor who doesn't have money? Would you hire a defense attorney who has no trial experience? Then why not be just as specific with choosing your

loan officer? This person will be guiding you in the biggest financial investment of your life. Make sure he or she is qualified.

4. Don't focus only on the rate, or you will get into trouble! We'll discuss that later, but the rate is just one of the relevant pieces of data. You must have a prepared list of questions about what you need to know so you can be engaged in the borrowing process.

5. Don't assume that just because your loan has been preapproved that there will be no obstacles along the way. There are always challenges in closing a loan. It is the job of your lender to have the foresight to see the challenges early enough to either avoid them or have a solid Plan B to navigate any obstructions.

CHAPTER 2

PROTECT YOURSELVES

Have you ever wondered why you can call five lenders and receive five different rates and five different monthly payments?

Have you ever wondered why when you're looking into refinancing your house, one lender can't answer any of your questions until you answer their questions? While the next lender will give you a quote before even asking how much your homeowner's insurance or your property taxes cost?

As a consumer, your number one priority is being prepared and knowledgeable in order protect yourself.

Avoiding the Most Common Pitfall and Understanding Advertised Rates

The most common pitfall is focusing only on the rate. Everyone wants to know, "Why don't I get the rates that I see advertised?"

First, the super low-interest rates that you see advertised could be for an adjustable rate mortgage, which requires a unique situation to be a good fit.

Or it might be for a 15-year amortization instead of the typical 30-year. I'm a huge advocate of 15-year loans because of the difference in the interest rate and the interest repaid over the life of that loan. However, 30-year loans tend to be the most affordable for the majority of people and are also a good choice.

So, we're circling back around to, "Why don't I get the rates that I see advertised?" Out of the 188 loans that I closed last year, less than 10 percent fit into the perfect package that advertised rates require. That means 90 percent of my customers did not fit into the ideal box for the advertised rates. How come?

If you go shopping for rates, 9 out of 10 times the published rate is based on the following:

- A 740 or better credit score.
- At least 30 percent down or more.
- Conventional financing, not FHA, VA, RD, or grant programs,
- A loan amount between $250,000 and $417,000,
- Typically paying one discount point to buy that rate and sometimes more than one.
- A 30-day rate lock—meaning you must close on or before that 30-day expiration.

What is a discount point? It is a percentage of your loan amount charged to you, in addition to normal closing costs to obtain a lower rate. Sometimes lenders might also charge origination points.

That is the beautifully packaged box you must fit into to receive the quoted rate. If any of those factors are outside that box, then you will get a different rate. Each loan type, loan term, grant, etc., in addition to the aspects mentioned above, will affect the rate or what lenders call "pricing."

Not Your Neighbors' Mortgage [1]

Let's say you and your neighbor are both buying a house. You are each buying the same price house and you're both putting 10 percent down. Everything in your file is identical—conventional financing, same income, you are essentially twins! Except for one little difference, your

---

[1] As an additional resource, I recommend reading "Why Was Jerry's Rate so Much Lower" by Ted Rod published by *Mortgage Daily News* on May 3rd 2016. It can be accessed at this URL: http://www.mortgagenewsdaily.com/channels/community/05032016-llpa-rates.aspx

neighbor's credit score is a 741 and yours is a 738. Guess what? You two likely aren't going to get the same rate, just because of a tiny difference. Just keep that in mind when understanding rates.

If you do decide that you want to call around for rates, don't just ask what rate is being offered. Tell the lender everything you know. "I'm going with an FHA loan. I want to put down 3.5 percent. My credit score is between 640 and 660. I am closing in 60 days. I want to purchase a house for $250,000, and I don't want to pay any points."

Be detailed. That way you can get the most accurate rate for your situation and you won't be surprised later with a rate change. Feel free to specify what is most important to you. For example, you might want the lowest closing cost or the lowest cash out of pocket, or maybe the rate is most important to you.

When my husband and I purchased our second house, I called at least 10 different lenders and, let me tell you, I shopped the rates! This was before I became a lender. It was the 1990s and, at that particular time, the interest rate for good credit was 6.875 percent, so that was my rate ... or so I thought!

We constructed a house and the lender had not explained to me about locking in interest-rate terms or rate lock expirations. After the house was built, she said, "It's time to lock in your interest rate." Well, of course, I was dramatically surprised. "What do you mean?" I asked. "Where's my 6.875 percent?" Then she told us that was the rate on a 30-day lock, but we had taken six months to build the house.

At that point, with good credit, the rates were 8 percent. Yes, 8 percent! I almost couldn't afford the house I had just spent six months building! Regarding the rates mentioned above: they're typically based on a 30-day lock, so the second that you need a different timeframe, the rate changes.

Mortgage rates are not like other loan rates. They can change daily and sometimes multiple times a day.

If you don't lock in the rate, it is subject to change until you do lock it in. Then, if you don't meet that closing date, you will incur lock extension fees because your loan can't be delivered in time. You can lock in on a purchase once you have a closing date and an executed contract. On a refinance, you can generally lock in once you have turned in your documents and paid for an appraisal.

A rate lock extension fee is not a "junk fee." It is not a way for a lender to make more money from you. It is a valid cost. When you're trying to get a quote, don't forget to say how long an interest rate lock you will need. Also, be aware of the rate lock expiration date in relation to your closing date.

Friendly Advice

You might notice that the second you say you're buying a house, everybody becomes an expert and wants to tell you how it all works. Just remember how drastically different everything can be just from one minor difference, so be aware that their experience will most likely *not be* your experience. Also remember this is not your neighbors' mortgage.

While everyone wants to give you advice, please know that in order to become a licensed mortgage loan officer who does not work for an FDIC insured bank, the officer has to pass an incredibly difficult exam. I would guess that at least 30 to 40 percent of people initially fail this test. Plus, there are continuing education courses required annually, along with multiple exams throughout the year to keep the license current.

So when everybody wants to advise you, just remember that they don't really know. It's like people telling you what stocks to buy and how to play the market, when they're not a licensed financial advisor.

For example, there was a grant program that gave the borrowers 5 percent of their loan amount toward closing costs, prepaid items, and down payment. Yes, it was actually "free money" that did not need to be repaid. However, there were additional charges that applied for that grant, about 1.6 percent in fees, that the borrowers wouldn't normally pay. But in the end, they were still getting 3.4 percent in free money!

I have had clients who saw the value in the program and understood that it didn't have to be repaid and that they were getting cash-to-close assistance "free money." Then they talked to various family members who convinced them that they were being ripped off by the fees so they walked away from 3.4 percent in free money.

My advice to you is to be diligent. Ask questions and have a clear understanding of what you're doing and why. Take the help that friends and family offer; just take it with a grain of salt if they're not a licensed professional.

Banks vs. Mortgage Companies vs. Mortgage Bankers

Another important topic to cover is the bank versus mortgage company versus mortgage banker discussion.

Many people think, "Oh, let me just call my bank; it already has my information, which is going to make it easier." Just know that your banker will require all the same paperwork as any mortgage company or lender. It will not be any less paperwork for you by going with your bank versus a different lender. It will be the same.

Banks are insured by the Federal Deposit Insurance Corporation (FDIC), and therefore their loan officers are exempt from the licensing requirements that govern loan officers at mortgage companies/mortgage brokers or mortgage bankers. They don't have to take that difficult test I told you about with the high failure rate and they're not required to have as much continuing education either. As strange as it seems, bankers are not as educated or qualified in the field of mortgage lending as loan officers at mortgage companies.

In fact, most banks hire their loan officers based on whether they're good at sales or not. That's really scary to me. In the United States, people take it way too lightly about references for mortgage loans. You want someone with knowledge and hands-on experience, not just a banker who's good at sales. Licensed loan officers have to know the complete file, the guidelines, and all the rules and regulations, whereas a bank loan officer might not.

At some FDIC banks, and other lending establishments, loan officers will just pass an application down the line—like throwing a noodle on the wall to see if it sticks! To me, that is not correct nor does it protect a consumer.

When closing a loan, loan officers often deal with entire families. Someone might have relocated to start a new job, or there might be children trying to start school who will be affected. There is also the domino effect of everyone involved in the closing. There are sellers, the title company, the insurance company, tax assessor, appraiser, inspector, processor, underwriter, auditor, etc. There are MANY lives affected. All of that needs to be taken seriously by a caring, well-trained, experienced professional who knows how to qualify you for a mortgage loan. You do not want to work with someone who is just taking a guess.

Buying a home is typically the largest purchase you will ever make. It is equivalent to the purchase of a car ten or twenty times over, and there is a lot involved. Therefore, you need to make an excellent informed decision about who's going to help you make the best choices for your financial situation.

You would not have someone prepare your taxes who wasn't licensed to prepare taxes. So, why would you hire a loan officer who wasn't licensed and who hasn't passed a comprehensive test?

Loans Are Like Snowflakes

We always say that every loan is like a snowflake, because no two are just alike.

If you go shopping for rates—like I did when I built my first house—just remember that every loan is like a snowflake and they're all dramatically different. That means you're not comparing apples to apples if you are just calling around and asking lenders for their rates without sharing the details of your individual situation.

Let's say you're offered a 1 percent interest rate and it's the most fantastic thing in the whole world. Just remember if you never get to a closing, the rate won't matter, and you'll have just wasted a lot of time. If it seems too good to be true, it is!

Instead, what you want are trustworthy referrals for loan officers. Ask your real estate agent for suggestions, find out who people you know have had good experiences with. Then have an open conversation with each of your options before deciding on your loan officer.

Loan Types

When it comes to getting a mortgage loan, homebuyers have fewer options than in the past, although there are still many options. From the early 2000s until 2008, lenders were willing to float exotic loans based on risky terms, but now we have returned to sensible home financing. Everything has to be verified, validated, tested, retested, and then audited. Be honest and direct with your loan officer from the beginning. This will ensure a smooth closing.

Fixed Rate vs. Adjustable Rate

With a fixed-rate home loan, your interest rate remains the same for the life of the loan duration. During a set duration, only a small portion of the payment pays the principal.

Whereas an adjustable-rate mortgage, or ARM, can change depending on the term, that is, 3, 5, 7, or 10 years.

Interest-only mortgage products, as the name implies, allow the option of paying only the interest for the first few years of the loan. These loans are usually adjustable rates.

In general, the longer you have the loan, the more principal you start to pay down from the beginning. The shorter the term, the less interest you pay.

What Type of Loan Do You Want?

There are so many ways to answer that question. Each loan has different guidelines and different requirements in terms of the down payment, monthly payment, debt-to-income ratio, housing ratios, and asset requirements. The important thing is that you know what type of questions should be asked and what types of topics should be discussed when deciding to choose a loan type.

Here are some examples of questions you should expect from a good loan officer:

- How much do you want to pay monthly?
- How much is your ideal down payment?
- How long do you plan on paying the mortgage?
- How long do you plan on living in the home?
- How much cash do you plan to bring to closing?

While you might decide it's a 20-year home, you might have plans that are unknown to your loan officer if you don't discuss it. For example, you might decide to rent the house in three years and keep it as an income property. Perhaps you have no desire to have a mortgage past 15 years, even though you might choose to start out with a 30-year term. Or maybe you only plan to live there for two years.

The answers to all these options make a great difference in choosing a loan type, loan term, and whether or not you want to pay points or additional fees for lower rates, or get closing cost/lender credit assistance, etc. It is truly case by case, so be detailed and be aware.

What Are My Mortgage Insurance Options?

PMI vs. MIP

Private mortgage insurance is sometimes called PMI or mortgage insurance premium (MIP)—different loan types have different names. Some clients assume that it's an insurance policy that protects them in case they pass away by paying their mortgage off. However, this is incorrect.

Mortgage insurance is an insurance policy that protects the lender in case the borrower defaults on the mortgage.

The only way to avoid paying PMI/MIP with conventional financing is on a purchase with 20 percent down, or on a refinance with 20 percent equity. While there's no way to avoid it otherwise, there are many conventional mortgage insurance options, most of which are never reviewed with the consumer. The options will vary depending on the qualifications and loan types and terms. Here are three suggestions.

1. There's monthly, which 9 out of 10 lenders offer. I find it is NOT usually the best or cheapest option.
2. There are also lender-paid mortgage insurance plans, where the mortgage insurance is built into the rate. You pay a higher rate, but you have no separate monthly mortgage insurance payment.
3. There's also single premium mortgage insurance, where you pay the mortgage insurance upfront in one lump sum but at a drastically reduced price, typically saving thousands of dollars in the process.

So if you know that you're not putting 20 percent down and you need mortgage insurance, make sure you're asking about the various options. An important note: Certain loan types only offer monthly PMI/MIP.

Depending on the loan type, some mortgage insurance is required, regardless of down payment, for the life of the loan. Yes, this is correct; some require it even with 20 percent down. Other mortgage insurance might potentially fall off automatically when you're at 78 percent loan to value. Once you're at 80 percent loan to value, you can call or write and request the mortgage insurance be removed on certain loan types. Some programs have life-of-the-loan mortgage insurance.

Be sure to reference your Truth in Lending Act (TILA) document as well as your amortization schedule, as those two documents will give you the exact dates as to when the 78 percent automatically happens or when you have that opportunity to make that request at 80 percent, if it applies to your loan type. Talk to your accountant, because there might even be tax advantages of one mortgage insurance over another.

Another good question is, "Will your lender shop multiple mortgage insurance companies?" I shop several mortgage insurance companies for my clients to find the best deal for their specific situations at the best possible price.

So for mortgage insurance, we have monthly, we have single, and we also have lender paid. Be sure to know your options and ask the right questions before making your decision.

Home Insurance

Home insurance requires you to think about unpleasant occurrences: floods, disasters, and emergency home repairs. While it might seem pessimistic to dwell on what negative events could happen, it's important to protect yourself from some of life's biggest surprises.

When it comes to protecting your home, it's not just about safeguarding against structural damage or theft—it's just as much about feeling secure where you live. If disaster strikes, your focus should be on reclaiming your sense of stability. The last thing you should have to worry about is money. The lenders must also protect their interest. Adequate home insurance, sometimes called hazard insurance, is always a lender requirement. Flood insurance might also be required.

Property Taxes

The property tax is a levy on the value of a privately owned property. In most states this includes land. Property tax liability is calculated by multiplying the nominal property tax rate by the assessment ratio (the percentage of the value of the property that is taxed) by the value of the property. In some states, people might get a homestead exemption and are not taxed on the full value. In some states, additional taxes apply.

On a purchase, it's important to realize it's usually *irrelevant* what the seller pays. I'll repeat that. Do not expect to pay the same property tax amount that the seller pays. You need your lender to calculate based on your purchase price. The amount almost always differs between the buyer and the seller.

Flood Insurance

If your home is damaged in a flood, are you covered? That depends on the value of your home, the level of water damage, and whether or not you have flood insurance.

If it's determined that you are in an "A" zone, your lender will require flood insurance. Regular homeowner's insurance policies don't cover flood damage. Typically, flood insurance can be transferred, while home insurance never can. If the home is located in a B, C, or X zone, flood insurance is generally not required.

Loan Term

A loan term is easy to identify. For example, a 30-year, fixed rate mortgage has a term of 30 years. However, loans can last for any number of years—as long or as short as a lender and borrower agree. Typically, there are 10, 15, 20, or 30-year mortgages, but options will vary by loan type and depending on the lender.

Conventional vs. FHA vs. VA vs. RD Loans

Monthly

Let's discuss monthly payment. Remember, your monthly payment consists of principal, interest, and escrow. Also, you usually have property taxes, home insurance, mortgage insurance, sometimes city taxes, and sometimes flood insurance, which accounts for the "escrow."

Typically, the only time you can choose to waive escrow and only pay principal and interest is if you pay a fee AND you put down at least 20 percent or have at least 20 percent equity—assuming this option is available on your loan type. Some loan types will not allow escrow waiving under any circumstances.

If you visit a website that supposedly estimates payments for you, be sure that it includes all these pieces to the puzzle. I can't tell you how many times clients have come to me only to find out that they have been looking in a dramatically wrong price range, based on misinformation from the Internet. Escrows tend to be left out of online equations or are drastically inaccurate in the estimates.

Cash to Close

This is different from closing costs, prepaid items, or the down payment. It is a combination of everything. It consists of your down payment, prepaid items, and closing costs. I remember meeting with a client and his loan officer had emailed him saying, "Your cash to close is $2,322." I went through everything with him line by line and pointed out the fact that the $2,322 was the difference between the closing costs total minus the $5,000 the seller was paying.

The loan officer had neglected to add the $5,600 down payment, making the estimated cash to close about $5,600 wrong. Had that client not spoken with me, and if I hadn't gone through everything line by line, he would have been in for the shock of his life on closing day. Unfortunately, this is not uncommon.

Escrows

Above and beyond your principal and interest payment, you might have an escrow account. About 9 out of 10 clients I work with have an escrow account.

Escrows are your prepaid taxes and insurance as well as mortgage insurance. If your home insurance is $1,200 a year vs. $1,210, $1,500, or $2,400, that changes your cash to close as well as your monthly payment.

An escrow account is another way that loan officers can misinform you of your numbers. They must ask when your insurances and taxes renew in order to be accurate.

Always remember one number on a home loan changes *all* the numbers. As an example, a $1,000 versus $1,200 tax bill changes your monthly payment and your cash to close.

Refinancing

Why do the numbers change drastically? This is a common question. My response is that it is the loan officers' job to do their absolute best to anticipate correct numbers for clients.

One of the main questions I hear regarding refinancing is that the lender will quote numbers to the client and use the balance of the existing mortgage from the credit report.

Every experienced loan officer should know the balance is not a payoff and that the payoff is higher than the balance. If this isn't clarified to the clients, they will be surprised at closing with higher than expected numbers.

On a refinance, in order to have a clear idea to figure out estimated prepaid items due at closing, the lender must know when the taxes and insurances come due or renew.

Here's a general idea to estimate prepaid items on a refinance: Take the month your first payment is due, in relation to the month when the bill is due, take the number 15 and then subtract the difference. So if your payment is due in January, and your bill (insurance/tax) is due in December, you'll take 11 payments from 15, which means that you would collect four months of escrow payments for that particular item.

Here are some common topics that you want to make sure are covered if you're trying to refinance.

If the loan officer is running numbers for you, then he or she should be asking for this information:

- The amount of your property taxes
- How much you pay for home insurance
- If you have flood insurance, and, if so, how much it costs
- The amount of your city taxes

If the loan officers aren't asking these questions and more, then they are giving you completely inaccurate numbers for your monthly payment as well as your cash at closing. Make sure to give them all the necessary information.

Once you are given the monthly payment amount, be sure to ask if it includes escrows and mortgage insurance.

When you're provided with your cash-to-close amount, ask if the down payment, closing costs, and prepaid items are included.

The Importance of Transparency

Last year, I submitted 190 loans to underwriting. I'm proud to say that 188 of those closed. The regrettable thing is that the two loans that were denied in underwriting were both business owners who refused to provide me with the documents I requested.

I had asked for all their personal and business tax returns, because they both owned more than 25 percent of their particular businesses. When you own more than 25 percent of a business, then we must look at the business tax returns in addition to the personal. If you own less, then we don't look at business tax returns.

In addition to those tax returns, I needed all the K-1s, W-2s, and 1099s that went with them. In both instances, the clients insisted the paperwork did not exist or that I did not need it. They fought the process, so rather than finding out on day one that they wouldn't be approved, they found out weeks into the process, which cost them time, money, and stress.

Every piece of the puzzle is essential, and it's always better to put everything on the table in the beginning. Missing pieces equal no loan.

It might be a bit of a stretch to say this, but when you're holding back documents from your lender, it's almost as if you're a drug addict at a doctor's appointment. You're doing drugs, but you're trying not to let the doctor know. However, once the doctor reviews the lab report, you can't lie and say you didn't take those drugs. The loan process is that detailed. Whatever you're trying to hide will be found out and it will cost you. It might be weeks and thousands of dollars into the process.

Please be transparent and don't fight the process.

If you'd like to learn more, Mark Greene wrote a great article called "The Perfect Loan File." It was published in *Forbes* on March 9, 2012. You can check it out at this URL:

http://www.forbes.com/sites/moneybuilder/2012/03/09/the-perfect-loan-file-2/#433c2aad6537

CHAPTER 3

PEACE OF MIND

Needless to say, people are always worried about the outcome of the process. Are they getting in the home before the baby comes? Are they getting in the home before they're married or after their wedding? Will they get in the home before or after their other place sells, or before or after their divorce is finalized? Will they move into the house in time for the kids to get registered for school? The list of concerns goes on and on.

Having peace of mind and being calm and confident is so important in this process, because every homebuyer is worried about the outcome. They all want to make sure that we're meeting that deadline of closing, regardless of their situation.

I had clients who came into the office, and they referred to themselves as being married. Here in the South, when you're together with someone and you live with them for so long, a lot of people sometimes just say "my husband" or "my wife," but on paper, they're not legally married.

So, this seemingly married couple meets with me, and they want to get a VA loan. We're going through the process, when the title work reveals that they are not legally married. I called them frantically, because VA loans have a unique condition that stipulates that you cannot borrow money with someone who is not your spouse, unless he or she is also a veteran.

At this point, we were two weeks into the four-week process. I started looking at everything quickly to see if the "husband," who was the veteran, could qualify on his own. The "wife" couldn't qualify on her own because she wasn't a veteran.

Then the couple says, "You know what? We'll get married. We were going to do it anyway. We'll get married tomorrow at the justice of the peace."

My assistant and I immediately offered to attend as their witnesses, because number one, that would be super awesome, and number two, we'll do whatever we can to remain within the guidelines and compliant to help meet a client's goals of homeownership!

They got married, we updated their whole file, and got them to an on-time closing. It was really exciting!

What I urge other lenders to do is to help the clients remain calm and confident and try to approve the file from the beginning and not at the end. That way we're not just waiting to see if the loan's going to go to a closing. Instead, we're working to ensure a smooth closing from the beginning.

A lot of this process lies in the hands of you, the borrower. I urge you to be diligent. The solution is quickly getting the loan officers all the paperwork they need.

As you can see from the stories I've shared already, your success is the result of a lot of the same things: getting the paperwork in on time; being clear and concise and not fighting the process, even during the moments when you might not understand it; and being completely transparent.

When all those things line up, they result in closings that happen quickly and smoothly, with happy customers—buyers and sellers.

CHAPTER 4

THE ULTIMATE UNDERSTANDING OF THE UNDERWRITING PROCESS, WITH THE END GOAL IN MIND: A SMOOTH AND PEACEFUL TRANSACTION

Do you remember the Rubik's Cube? The purpose of the game was to get solid colors on each side of the 3D puzzle. Do you remember how many steps it took and what a big deal it was to achieve that goal? The underwriting process is similar. Everything needs to line up correctly for your loan to go through smoothly. And just like the Rubik's Cube, it takes patience, accuracy, detail, and hard work.

Roles

Let's talk about various roles in the loan process.

1. Loan officer—You have a loan officer who is there to be the advocate for the consumer and gather all the information for the file. That information typically goes through a process called "scrubbing or processing," before it ever gets to an underwriter. The underwriter's job is to review the file. Ideally, it's already put together, and all the

underwriter has to do is just check off all the boxes. That would be in the perfect world of mortgage lending!

Unfortunately, the mortgage industry is not perfect; it's broken. Most loan officers do not have the training, education, or guideline experience to know how to handle all those pieces and parts—like all the squares of a Rubik's Cube. If they don't have this knowledge, then things won't line up, and you might not get the loan.

2. Processor—After the loan officer, it goes to the processor. The processors many companies have are not trained to underwrite a file, so they do what they can to put the file together before passing it to the underwriter. They gather the information and build the file, but they do not always analyze the data prior to providing it to the underwriter.

3. Underwriter—If there are any problems or missing pieces with the file, the underwriter will catch them. However, I believe the loan officer or the processor should flag any issues before the file reaches the underwriter. So again, you must make sure you are choosing the best loan officer or team.

If the underwriter does find a problem, he or she might request more information or simply say the loan can't be approved. The problem with this is that the underwriter probably won't get your file until you're anywhere from two to four weeks into the process.

So there you are, the homebuyer, thinking that you're near the end of the process, and all of a sudden here comes the underwriter with all kinds of questions.

I'm an advocate of the system we use at my company. We train the loan officers and the processors to pre-underwrite the file. That way when the file goes to underwriting, there is one review and the loan is approved! We call it "one and done" lending.

According to the national average, when a loan officer submits a file to an underwriter, the underwriter typically has a list of a 12–17 missing items for each file. The average in my office is less than two items because of the process that we use. My goal is to see a "one and done" system in place across the country. This would transform the industry.

Now let's further discuss the role of the underwriters. What do they want? What do they do? The underwriter is looking at four things: capacity, assets, collateral, and credit.

Underwriting to Capacity

This is an analysis of not only your income but also your assets and your likeliness to pay. It's a review of your debt-to-income ratio, meaning how much money is going in and how much money is going out, in percentages.

Here are some of the things the underwriter is reviewing:

- What percentage of your income is your housing payment? How does that relate to all your other expenses?
- Do you make enough money to sustain the loan?

What's important to know is that there are four different types of income:

1. There is the income that your employer pays you.
2. There is your net income: the money that you can physically put into your pocket or "cash in hand" income.
3. There is adjusted gross income, which is the income that the IRS taxes.
4. There is qualifying income for a mortgage loan.

These four rarely match and one is never consistently higher or lower than another is.

The underwriter, or if you're lucky, the loan officer and processor, use your W-2s, 1099s, K-1s, tax returns, and your four most recent check stubs to review your income. The underwriter also requests verification from the IRS for the tax returns and the W-2s. The underwriter also gets written verification from your employers, past and present.

Then the underwriter compares all the documents, line by line, to make sure that everything is perfectly congruent. It is analyzed, reanalyzed, and reverified.

Sometimes this process leads to more questions. For instance, perhaps your tax return says you made $50,000 in W-2 income, and you provided three W-2s that equal $50,000, so it looks like everything's fine. However, the IRS W-2 transcripts show $52,100 in W-2 income, because you worked at a job for a month and forgot to report it on your taxes or to the lender. Now you have incorrect, incomplete taxes, and we have a red alert on the file and a potential impasse. See why when we say we need all the W-2s, we mean all of them? The details are everything.

Let's put that to the side for a minute and assume that the figures all match perfectly. Then the underwriter is going to take the W-2s and the tax returns and match them up with the paycheck stubs. Then he is going to request verification—a breakdown directly from the employer. Everything has to match exactly, but to be honest it rarely does; so then the lender must connect the dots and find a way to match it all up.

When it doesn't match, it leads to more questions and more paperwork to fill in the holes. All that work goes into calculating how much money the borrower makes. Keep in mind this is assuming that the borrower has all of the tax returns, W-2s, and paycheck stubs available. Also this is the "easy" income process for a W-2 employee. We will go into other income types later, as they are usually more complicated.

Obviously, all this takes time. It can take weeks for the IRS to give us transcripts. It can take an employer anywhere from just a few hours to multiple weeks to verify employment verifications. Until every single piece is in, the loan officer/processor/underwriter can't accurately underwrite the income. If you've been diligent in choosing a loan officer, this will be completed at the beginning of your loan process, not the end, which is currently the industry standard.

Underwriting the Assets

Next, the underwriter is going to verify the assets. This is typically looking at liquid assets, which would be checking or savings accounts. The underwriter is also looking at other assets, such as 401(k) or 403(b) retirement savings plans, individual retirement accounts (IRA), stocks, bonds, mutual funds, and certificates of deposit (CD). The underwriter reviews the information from two angles. First, he wants to know if you have enough cash to close. Second, he wants to see how many months of reserves you have available.

Reserves are the assets remaining after closing. How much money can be accessed immediately if something goes wrong and you need fast money to pay your mortgage? The underwriter assesses how many months' payments you could pay with this money from savings before defaulting on the loan.

If you have checking and savings accounts containing all your assets, then it's a simple assessment. Typically, you'll only need to provide two months of bank statements covering at least 60 days, most recent and consecutive.

The underwriter is looking to see if there are any non-sufficient fund (NSF) checks or bank charges in the account history. He will analyze every page of the bank statement, even if it's blank. Clients are always asking, "Why do you need it, if it's a blank page?" For all we know, that blank page could show that you have a loan against all the money in that account. Every single page must be provided and analyzed.

Then your 401(k), 403(b), IRAs, stocks, bonds, or CDs are analyzed. The client might say, "I have ten thousand dollars." Okay, maybe you have ten thousand in a 401K, but are you vested? Maybe you don't have access to that ten thousand. Or perhaps you are vested at ten thousand, but there are taxes and penalties for early withdrawal, leaving you only six thousand dollars.

The underwriter has to show proof of all the terms and liquidations for all the assets, even if you don't plan on taking that money out for cash to close. So you might have an account with $10K, but your loan application is updated to reflect a $6K balance because the full amount cannot be accessed. Some program guidelines require a certain percentage be used.

Underwriting for Collateral

Now the underwriter is going to underwrite for collateral "property." The appraisal will be reviewed. The value noted will be viewed at a sales comparison approach versus a cost approach. He is going to look at comparables provided on the appraisal. If a comparable is listed for sale but not yet sold, it'll be looked at, but it's not going to be considered as heavily as a comparable house that is already sold. The comparables must be similar and valid. The adjustments made to value must be acceptable and in range. The land value versus the dwelling value needs to be within guidelines. The condition must meet guidelines. Are the comparables within an acceptable distance of each other?

Keep in mind that people can list their home for any price they wish. They can make up the price because they "feel" it's worth that much. What matters is what it sells for and what the market bears. Is the appraisal valid? Are the comparables accurate? Is the property in good condition? Is it marketable? Can it be insured adequately? Are there hazards to consider?

Underwriting for Credit

- Based on your credit history, are you likely to repay in a timely fashion?
- How is your credit history?
- How many late payments have you had? How recent are they? What types of accounts were late?
- Do you have revolving credit? Have you used a lot of that revolving credit?
- Do you show that you're responsible or are your credit cards maxed out?
- Will the loan be sellable?
- Does the loan fit into one of the many boxes available?
- Does it meet the guidelines?

Analysis Overview

We've addressed capacity, assets, collateral, and credit.

Imagine that you have a stool with four legs. If a leg is missing, it is going to topple over. It's the same thing with the loan process. If one of the four items isn't solid, then your loan will not be approved. There are some exceptions to the rule, because there are different loan products for various property types with certain qualifications.

I had a borrower whose file looked perfect, but then it turned out that two months before applying for the loan, her employer had switched her from salary to commission. All the check stubs that we reviewed showed commission, but she was paid a salary before then. As an example, when the borrower is 100 percent commission, I need to show stability. That *generally* requires two years of consecutive commission history.

There are some rare exceptions to the general rule, but it is usually 24 months of commission on average to look at the history to determine stability. Different forms of income require various types of proof of stability.

So even though everything else in her file was immaculate, that one shift could have meant she wouldn't be approved. Because with a two-month, 100 percent commission history, she has zero income in a lenders' eyes. Luckily, in her case, we were able to add a co-borrower, and it all worked out.

CHAPTER 5

DIFFERENT TYPES OF INCOME: YOU NEED *WHAT* DOCUMENT FROM ME?

Self-Employed Borrowers

If you're self-employed, there's a lot more analysis that goes into underwriting that part of your file.

When you are a W-2 employee, you typically have a set hourly rate or salary, unless you work on commission. However, when you're self-employed, your income can fluctuate wildly. Therefore, a lender looks two years back at taxable income to determine projections forward as to what the consistency of your income is going to be.

Put simply, when you're an employee, you get check stubs. Those can be compared to tax returns, to W-2s, and to verifications from the IRS and the employer. It is assumed the company you work for is stable and your job is likely to continue.

When you're self-employed, how the lenders verify your income depends on how you structure your self-employment. You might file a limited liability corporation (LLC) or a sole proprietorship. You might have a partnership, an S Corporation, or a C Corporation. Perhaps you provide a W-2 for yourself or use a K-1. Some business owners have an S Corp or a C Corp, where they have anywhere from 1 to 100 percent ownership.

The percentage of ownership will determine if the lender will require copies of your business tax returns in addition to copies of your personal tax returns. That will be in addition to all the verifications, check stubs, etc., that are always required.

There are many different ways that income for self-employed borrowers can be calculated, which is why it's so challenging. There is no one, simple way to say, "This is how we calculate how much money you make." The calculations are complex, and, again, we must have all the pieces we need.

There is always an exception to the rule, but generally speaking you need to have been self-employed for two sets of taxes. That might not mean two years; it means two tax returns.

Some self-employed borrowers feel frustrated by the process and level of scrutiny. They often remark that there's no more of a guarantee that their business will fail, leaving them out of a job versus someone being fired from any other company. There is some truth to that.

However, what's important to know is some of the statistics that lenders have to take into consideration: **Roughly, 40 percent of self-employed businesses fail in the first year. Projecting from year one to year five and the end of five years, that's less than 10 percent of businesses that have actually survived.**

The lender has to take all those risks into consideration to make the determination of the stability and likelihood of continuance of that income. This means that self-employed borrowers are analyzed a little more heavily than a W-2 employee is.

Sometimes borrowers say, "I have an S Corp or a C Corp, and I W-2 myself, so I only want you to look at my W-2s and check stubs because

I'm an employee of my company." The key to that statement is that it is *your* company, which means we need to look at all the pieces of your puzzle. You can't pick and choose what income you want to use to qualify. It all has to be analyzed.

Lenders need to see all your income documentation. If I'm able to qualify you based solely on your W-2s, and there is income that I can document but might not use to qualify, then that can be done under certain circumstances.

The main point is, please do not be discouraged as a self-employed borrower to apply for a loan. You are not at any disadvantage.

Issues can arise when someone claims a lot of income and takes a lot of deductions. For example, you can't tell the IRS you made $1,000,000, but only $100,000 was taxable because of all your deductions, and then turn around and go to a lender and say, "I made $1,000,000." That won't work. Depending on your returns, you might have qualifying income of $200K, even though the gross was $1 million and the adjusted gross was $100K.

It's important to remember that the way your lender thinks and how your accountant thinks rarely align! Certified public accountant (CPA) regulations are not lender regulations or guidelines and vice versa.

Unsuccessful Self-Employed Stories

I've had numerous successes with self-employed borrowers, but here is an example of an unsuccessful ending.

I had a borrower who kept denying that he had a K-1 for a particular company. I repeatedly explained that he must have one, based on a line item in his tax returns.

He argued for weeks that he didn't have a K-1 until finally, at the end of his process, he gave in and provided that documentation. Unfortunately, his loan was denied. If I had that K-1 from day one, I would never have had him proceed forward with the contract, appraisal, or inspection. His lack of full transparency cost him time, money, and heartache.

Sometimes based on credit and verbal information, self-employed borrowers are told by lenders that they will qualify for a loan. Then when the underwriter analyzes the self-employment income, it's revealed to be nowhere near the qualifying income for a list of reasons. Make sure you choose a loan officer who will ask the right questions and request the right documents in order to accurately analyze your qualifying income.

In many cases, the borrowers have already spent money on everything required (appraisal, inspections, etc.) to move forward with owning their dream house, only to find out later that they've been denied.

Often borrowers don't understand why they need to provide the documents they've been asked for, or they think something does not matter and so they refuse to provide the requested documents. In either case, it can be detrimental to their files.

Self-Employed Success Stories

I have so many success stories of self-employed borrowers who had previously been denied, but later I was able to get them approved.

In most cases, the lenders did not adequately analyze the self-employment income, because they found it overwhelming and complicated. Finding knowledgeable lenders is crucial. Ask about their experience with self-employed borrowers. Are they asking for all the pieces of the puzzle I have mentioned to you? If they say, "Everything looks good to me," before analyzing your documents, you need to ask questions.

Here are a few interview questions to consider:
- How many loans did you close last year?
- Tell me about your process.

- How long have you been originating home loans?
- Do you have experience with self-employed borrowers? How much?
- At what point does the file go to underwriting?

Their answers will make a difference to your success. Be sure to choose wisely.

One time a client called me and just started rattling things off. "I have this business, this business, and that business. And this other business is the parent company of this business. And I own this other company with these two other people."

I wrote down his whole spiel and repeated it back to him. He was speechless. He told me that he'd spoken with four lenders and none of them had been able to follow him. I explained that I have a lot of experience with self-employed borrowers, because I enjoy challenges and finding solutions.

He was lovely to work with, but we ended up having to deny his loan. I explained to him why we couldn't help him, but that some of the regulations would be changing in the next tax year in his favor.

You might be thinking, how is this a success story? Well, there are two parts to this success story.

First, it is uncommon for a client to send a lender a gift, and it is especially rare for a client to send a gift when their loan was denied! But he sent my office a gorgeous bouquet of roses with a note expressing his appreciation for our time and the overall way we handled everything. It was wonderful to be acknowledged in that way.

Then, about six months later, after the new regulations were in place and he had filed his tax return, we were able to finance his home.

It was so exciting to find the best solution for him and eventually meet his goals while educating him on how the process works, which allowed him to protect himself in the future. This is just one example of how knowledge and persistence pays off for the borrower and the lender.

Different Types of Income

There are many types of income, including, but not limited to, the following:

- Alimony
- Annuity
- Capital gains
- Cash (if reported to the IRS)
- Child support
- Disability
- Dividend and interest income
- Military benefits
- Military pay
- Notes receivable
- Pension
- Real estate rental investment properties
- Retirement
- Royalties
- Social security

How these are all calculated will vary, depending on the specifics of each situation. What's important is to remember to disclose any and all types of income to your lender.

Keep in mind that cash sources of income do not exist in the eyes of the lender unless they are reported to the IRS; neither do other types of income that is not reported to the IRS.

Sometimes child support and alimony can be counted as income from day one and sometimes you need to prove six months' receipts of these payments. There are even cases where you might have to show continuous receipt, without cessation, for twelve months. The payments will need to continue for at least three years, and that will have to be validated through paperwork. Your lender will ask for previous divorce decrees because the decree will state all the terms. The lender might even need birth certificates, etc. Just remember to provide all pages of all documents.

Please note that forgetting to disclose that you pay child support or alimony might change your approval. If you take a while to give the lender your judgments from a divorce decree, then you might discover that you've been working with an invalid approval that will turn into a denial once all the paperwork is in.

Another important thing to note is this—if you work for your family, be sure to disclose that right away, as additional documentation will likely to be needed. A lot of clients wonder why this matters. It is viewed that if your income is derived from family, the likeliness of fraud increases.

Even if you don't tell the lender about your alimony or child support payments, it might be revealed in a credit report, check stubs, or another document. As I've said before, it all comes out in the process.

CHAPTER 6

A WINNING TEAM

What most people do not realize is how many people are involved in closing a mortgage loan.

- Lender-loan officer
- Lender's team
- Processor
- People who perform verifications
- Underwriter
- Underwriter's team
- Auditor
- Closer
- Appraisal department
- Funder
- Title company
- Notary
- Attorney
- Clerk
- Abstractor
- Home inspector
- Home insurance agent
- Appraiser/home warranty company
- Flood insurance agent

- Tax assessor
- Home association
- Condo association
- One to two real estate agents

It truly takes a village of people from the beginning to the end of the process!

What you need to look for is a winning team from the lending side, because without that you could be set up for failure. Think of the lender as the conductor of an orchestra. All the musicians are highly trained and talented individuals, but they still need the conductor to lead them in bringing out the full beauty of the music. Every person involved in the mortgage process is an integral part of the team, but you need a lender who is an excellent captain.

Characteristics of a Winning Team

Here are a few things I want you to look for to find the right fit for your team.

Attention to Detail

Number one, they must have attention to detail—and I mean to every detail.

Just as one example, if they don't ask about your plans for that home, for example, how many years you plan to live there, then they really can't advise you as to what's best for you.

The answer to just this one question could make the difference in whether I suggest a conventional loan, a Federal Housing Administration (FHA) loan, a US Department of Veterans Affairs (VA) loan, a US Department of Agriculture Rural Development (RD) loan, or whatever might apply.

That kind of attention to detail can make a huge difference to you as a consumer—we're talking thousands and thousands of dollars between upfront, lifetime, and monthly expenses. Your long-term and short-term goals need to be discussed.

Does your loan officer review your complete situation and advise what's best for you? Or does he just take orders? If you walk in and say, "I want an FHA loan," you do not want someone who just says, "Okay."

Ideally, the loan officer will talk to you about why you want what you want. He should make sure you understand it completely and review all the pros and cons with you.

He should ask questions, such as the following:

- What are your goals for this property?
- Do you plan to live in it for two years, five years, or ten years?
- Do you plan on keeping it forever?
- Might you potentially turn it into investment property some time later?
- How long do you plan to take to pay it off?

Does he take in your overall financial picture and say, "You want to put $50,000 down on your home, but I see that you have $10,000 outstanding on a credit card at 25 percent interest. Maybe we should put $40,000 down on the home and get that credit card paid off to put you in a better overall position."

It is imperative to discuss details. As a consumer, you don't know what you don't know. Even if you're incredibly savvy, it's still the loan officer's job to ask the right questions and make sure that you're making the best decision for you.

You also want someone who will work diligently to ensure that all your numbers are as accurate as possible. For example, that means confirming the closing fees with the title company or the quote given by your home insurance agent. That is why attention to detail means so much. You want someone who treats your money the way they would treat their own or better!

Here's an example of why attention to detail matters so much. There was a client who wanted a $200,000 VA loan for a $240,000 home. Many lenders denied him or told him he had to get a less expensive home because of his debt-to-income ratio.

By paying attention to detail, it was revealed that he had more than $20,000 in credit card debt, at high interest rates with high minimum payments. So he was advised to borrow $220,000 instead of $200,000 and take the additional $20,000 to pay off the credit cards. Then the debt was on a tax-deductible loan at a much better rate. The payments were paying down principal, whereas on the credit cards, it was just minimum payments. And he saved $200 a month by following that plan versus the original plan. Now the client is in an overall better situation and living in his dream home!

Paying attention to detail and having the kind of knowledge and expertise that comes from doing so many loans meant all the difference for that client. That makes me proud to be a part of changing his life.

I know of a borrower who wanted 100 percent financing. Everything looked beautiful, but the loan officer didn't look at the paycheck stubs carefully. Everything was moving ahead—the appraisal was done, the title was done, the inspections had been ordered.

Then two weeks into the process, the underwriter gets the paycheck stubs and says, "Wait a minute. There's a $400-a-month garnishment on the paycheck. What is that about?"

It turns out the borrower had a judgment against her and payments were being taken out of her checks with several more years to go before it would be repaid.

When that additional payment was added to the debt-to-income ratio, that borrower did not qualify for the home that she had just spent two weeks and roughly $1,500 on. Had the loan officer paid attention to detail, he would have caught that when the check stub was provided in beginning of the process.

Those are just two quick stories out of the thousands I've experienced that demonstrate how attention to detail makes all the difference in the world when it comes to your home financing. Because the consumers do not know what they do not know, they depend on the loan officer to take great care of them.

The loan officers should be someone who understands your needs, goals, and concerns. They need to care about you and your situation, including the timeline of your closing.

Experience

Your loan officer should be someone who is intimately acquainted with the loan process and will consider every option.

Not only do you want your loan officer to have general loan experience, but you also want him or her to have experience in different loan types. It's not just about how long the officer has been involved with loans, but how many deals he or she has done. Experience, along with hands-on knowledge, is an absolute must. Ask to hear the success stories and see if the loan officer is passionate when sharing them.

At FDIC-insured banks, loan officers don't even have to be licensed by the Nationwide Multistate Licensing System and Registry (NMLS). They often just take an application, pass it down the line, and see what happens. They don't analyze that application, and the corresponding documents, to make sure there is an excellent shot of the loan closing before they start collecting the client's money and probably wasting their time.

If loan officers work for a non-FDIC institution, such as a mortgage banker or mortgage lender, they must be NMLS licensed. The test is rigorous and the continuing education is grueling, but it protects the consumers and educates the loan officer. For some reason, loan officers at FDIC banks are exempt from this advantageous training and testing.

Vested Interest

Does the loan officer have a vested interest in your success? Does he have your best interest at heart? Will he analyze your entire situation?

My team and I have a vested interest in every client. We not only want you as our client for life, but we want you to have the confidence to wholeheartedly refer us to your friends and family, because you know that we will take care of them in every way possible.

My team has a vested interest, because we don't look at a client as a number or transaction. We look at the client as a person or a family member who has all their items packed on a truck and is expecting to get into a house on a particular day to start a new journey in their life. I know how many lives each transaction can affect. It's a domino effect.

We have a vested interest, because we feel honored to do this job. It still amazes me that I can work in a field where with every transaction I complete, I am helping to support a business, a person, and/or a family. I'm happy to be fulfilling my mission of changing the world one loan at a time.

I have a vested interest because I am the expert. You come to me so I can protect you from the things that you don't know you don't know.

Product Knowledge

Product knowledge is crucial. If I don't analyze every part of your file and determine what you truly qualify for, it can make or break a deal. Sadly, it is not uncommon for closing day to arrive and the buyer is told, "Oh, your debt-to-income ratio is too high for this program," or, "You don't have enough monthly savings for this program," or, "You don't have enough residual income for this program. You are not closing today."

All these issues could have and should have been discovered before closing day. If you're with a lender with expert product knowledge who pays attention to detail and has a vested interest in protecting you as a consumer, you shouldn't have any surprises at the end of the process, if you are transparent.

Guideline Knowledge

Buying a house might be the most complicated financial process of your entire life. As such, having a loan officer by your side who knows the ins and outs of the process and is well equipped with all the knowledge will help you out greatly.

Every home-buying experience is different, with its own twists and turns. An experienced loan officer will ease most of the pressure off you and ensure there aren't mishaps along the way.

There have been years when more than 300 changes took place to the lending guidelines in one calendar year. Therefore, loan officers need to stay up to date with the current loan guidelines and updates. Ask how often they read the guidelines.

Training

You want someone who prides themselves on their ongoing training.

You might want to ask, "How much training do you get throughout the year?"

Loan officers who are working on only one or two loans a month and are just taking the necessary requirements for their license will not have the most up-to-date knowledge. They just aren't equipped to take the best care of you.

Personally, I do the required hours, plus I travel out of state to four trainings a year. In addition to that, I read about three to four books a year on the industry. I also take the training courses offered by my company, which are usually once or twice a month, while also staying up to date on the guidelines.

I feel that it's important to continue learning, because things are always changing. If I don't adapt and don't learn, mistakes can be made, and my clients won't be protected.

Leadership

Look for a loan officer with leadership skills. The loan process requires direction and leadership. Imagine a symphony without the conductor. Would it work? Yes. Would it be fine? Perhaps. But would it be flawless and beautiful? Absolutely not.

A leader knows when it's time to stay the course or when the plan has to shift to arrive at the result that meets all the clients' goals. That takes leadership skills.

Leaders need to work with a sense of urgency in getting things accomplished for you and with an awareness of the importance of your closing date.

Communication

Ideally, the loan officers are excellent communicators who continually make sure everyone is on the same page. Every Tuesday, my team updates our clients. We're in contact much more than that, but we have a status call every Tuesday without fail. Communication is essential. Our clients always know where they stand. Remember, teamwork makes the dream work!

Sphere of Influence

You want a loan officer who has an excellent sphere of influence and a great reputation. He or she needs to be a person who can connect you with the right people to assist you through the process of your home purchase and/or your refinance. That could include, but is not limited to, a financial planner, a life insurance agent, a home warranty company, an alarm company, home insurance agent, a real estate agent, etc.

Team Members

Did you know that, on average, most loan officers close fewer than two loans in a month? That is not what I call experienced. Also, most loan officers do not have a team of people working with them to get everything completed for you.

You want a team that has many knowledgeable members who can answer your questions and keep things moving. It's also better for you if they offer additional services, like helping you shop for home insurance, or a home inspector, or Realtor. That's the kind of team you want.

Having the right team in place is crucial. Think of a garden hose; if there's even one kink in it, the water might drip out, but it will not be as efficient as it could be, and there's a chance it could become blocked altogether.

Recognition in the Market

Does your lender have recognition in the market? What is the feedback when you ask other people in the area about this lender? Ask your financial advisor, your Realtor, or your builder for referrals; they can all offer good feedback.

Customer Reviews

Do your research: Look up the lender with the Better Business Bureau and check out the ratings on Yelp and the feedback on Facebook. You can also access the NMLS website for more information, and it's always great to ask for references.

Some loan officers even keep a "brag book" that will be filled with thank-you notes and emails that clients have sent them. I like to keep these messages posted on the wall in my conference room. It's so exciting to go back and look at thankful clients I've been honored to serve.

Why Use a Realtor?

There is immense value in using the services of a licensed real estate agent. Fulltime agents are out and about on a constant basis. They are familiarizing themselves with various areas, numerous price points, and many property types. They'll help you narrow your search field much better than you would just driving around or searching online.

Unfortunately, there have been so many times when clients chose to not use a real estate agent. They come to me with questions that I am not licensed to answer. Without a Realtor, they're essentially on their own in that arena, doing random Internet research in an attempt to protect themselves.

A Realtor can help you with what inspections are suggested based on the area and property type. The real estate agent, on behalf of the buyers, protects the buyers and is their advocate in getting them the best possible deal. They can assist you in knowing market value and negotiations.

As a buyer, you do not pay your real estate agent; the seller pays the real estate agent's fee, so it costs you nothing to benefit from the Realtor's expertise.

Real estate agents abide by strict rules and regulations in protecting you. It is almost like they are your attorney, representing you in court—for free!

Your Lender's Area Footprint

Sometimes it's important to know the area footprint of the person you're considering as your lender. This way, if you change cities or states, one person can help you with all your potential home buying and refinance needs.

As an example, when you're looking for property close to the Mississippi/Louisiana line, make sure that your loan officer can finance in both states, if you are looking for homes in both. That way you don't end up having your credit pulled from two difference places depending on your decision. As of 2016, I am licensed in Louisiana, Alabama, Mississippi, Georgia, Florida, and Texas.

Personal Interests—You Want a Well-Rounded Person

This might seem to be an odd section and some people might think it's irrelevant. However, I suggest that you look at a person's interests and hobbies to determine if they are well rounded. Do the interests align with your values? Is this person someone you want to work intimately with for the next few weeks or months? If you don't feel a good connection with the individual, it might be wise to look elsewhere.

My interests are changing the world, helping people, health, fitness, Yoga, camping, and nutrition. I do CrossFit. I like to ride all-terrain vehicles (ATV) off road. I am social, dependable, and I have a can-do attitude. And most important, I am determined to "win" for my clients.

Questions to Ask Your Loan Officer about Your Loan Approval

Every question is critical. It's just like when you're going to your doctor; you have to tell the doctor every single medicine you're on, as it will affect everything else.

I joke with my clients and say, "Just pretend I'm your therapist. You have to tell me everything, because everything makes a difference." So remember, details, details, details!

If you think to yourself, "Oh, that's small; that doesn't matter," red alerts should go off in your head. It's much better to err on the side of too much information versus too little, too late.

So here are some of my suggested questions about details. You need to get deeper than this, but here are some general points to remember:

- What is my loan term?
- Does my loan have a prepayment penalty?
- What is my loan type? Why? How is that best for me?
- Do I have mortgage insurance? Is it for the life of the loan?
- What will I repay over the life of my loan between principal and interest repayments?
- How do you find the best loan for me?
- Do you guarantee closing dates?
- What is your average number of days from contract to cleared to close? Not how many days from contract to close, but how many days from contract to cleared to close?

Why Is My Payment Different than Expected?

This is a common question for borrowers. I'm going to give you some points as to why this can happen:

- Escrows
- Down payment
- Loan type
- PMI vs. MIP
- Home insurance
- Property taxes
- Flood insurance
- Loan term

All these things can affect the monthly payment. There are a lot of moving parts, and if any of those things change in the process, it will change your expected payment.

To wrap up, remember that you want a loan officer who's diligent, has a vested interest in your success, and is incredibly detailed. All of this is imperative for your protection.

CHAPTER 7

CLOSING—THE MOVING TRUCK

Whoever would have thought a moving truck could have such a significant impact on anyone's life? The stories and situations that revolve around the moving truck can be stressful, exciting, and sometimes even quite comical.

Some of the things a client might worry about are these:

- Will I close on time?
- Can I schedule my moving truck?
- Will I be in a position where I've sold my other place, or given notice to the property owner, and have nowhere to go?
- If the closing is pushed back, what am I going to do with all my belongings on a truck?
- The moving truck costs "X" dollars; if the closing is late, that could mean a lot of additional costs to extend the rental.

In a way, the closing is entirely geared around that truck.

The crazy thing about closing contracts is that in the beginning, without having even started the process, the buyers, sellers, and Realtors determine a closing date.

Now, as you know, getting to the closing date is difficult. It's challenging because you don't know if the appraisal will come in late, or if there are going to be inspection issues, or how long collecting all the documents will take.

Lenders like to say that having a closing, or trying to get to a closing, is like orchestrating a circus. We are trying to get so many people from various areas to come together and meet a host of deadlines, so we can finally arrive at our shared goal called the closing date. It truly takes a village!

The next big questions that go along with the moving truck are, "I have a moving truck, and I'm going to this closing. What is about to happen to me? Who will be there? What can I expect?"

Who Attends the Closing?

Here's a list of who typically attends the closing:

- Your lender—although it isn't always possible for him or her to make it, but if they can, it could even take place in their office.
- Your title attorney—often the closing takes place at a title or escrow company.
- Your real estate agent—closing could also be held at the Realtor's office.
- The seller's real estate agent and the seller might be there—sometimes the appointments are staggered so that the seller comes in later and the buyer can complete his or her loan documents in private.

It usually takes about an hour to sign and go through all the paperwork. A lot of the paperwork is going to appear redundant, but it's all needed for funding the loan.

Mostly the closing is super exciting! In most states, you leave with the keys to the house, although in some states you don't.

The entire process will usually take an hour or less. And you will drive off in your moving truck, headed to your brand-new home to start the next chapter of your life!

By following the guidance in this book and having clear, avid communication with your lender, you can avoid closing surprises.

CHAPTER 8

IN CONCLUSION

I have a lofty goal—I want to change the world one loan at a time through helping clients and anyone who reads this book.

This goal cannot be met through me alone, but it can be met through other lenders who employ the same processes that I've proven will work.

Luckily, there are a lot of great lenders out there. I wish you all the best in finding one. I feel confident that I have shared all the tools and guidance you need to succeed.

The mortgage industry is a multibillion-dollar industry that affects so many lives. My hope and my determination are that this book helps people avoid mortgage mistakes, meltdowns, challenges, drama, and delays.

I know that this industry can be better, and I know that it is getting better. I hope that this book positively affects many people, not only the consumers, but also the lender and the Realtors. My hope is to help and inspire others.

For real estate agents, I hope this gives them a better understanding of the overall process, and helps them better serve and advise their customers to put them in the hands of the right lenders when they're asked for a reference. After all, a mortgage is a big commitment.

For consumers, I want you to have a better, happier, timely, and drama-free mortgage experience. To have *Mortgage Peace with a Smooth and On-Time Closing.*

For the world to change one loan at a time, it's going to need all of us to do our part. Just doing that one little part will make the biggest difference to so many other people. Your part is to be knowledgeable, be prepared, be diligent, and share this book with others!

Oftentimes, lenders get referrals because people like them. And that's good, of course. You want to like the person you work with. But I hope we all remember that it's about a lot more than just liking someone. This is your home, your life, and your dream.

You are referring others to a lender who is going to advise them on potentially the largest purchase of their life. Buying a home is a huge responsibility, with the potential for the most enduring adverse effects.

So make sure when you're referring your friends or your clients, that you're sending them to a responsible, diligent, detailed, and extremely knowledgeable lender. Be confident that the lender will accurately assess the overall financial picture of the buyer and will take care of that person by obtaining the mortgage that best suits the clients' needs. Be sure that the loan officer will adhere to the highest ethics and that he or she understands they are not there just to take an order.

Whether you're buying or refinancing a home, or if you're a Realtor making a referral, I invite you to check out my website: www.stephanieweeks.com.

Thank you for reading, and I hope I have helped you in some way.

www.ingramcontent.com/pod-product-compliance
Lightning Source LLC
Chambersburg PA
CBHW061215180526
45170CB00003B/1014